THE POWER OF NATURE

VOLCANOES

Arthur Gullo

Cavendish
Square

New York

Published in 2015 by Cavendish Square Publishing, LLC
243 5th Avenue, Suite 136, New York, NY 10016

Website: cavendishsq.com

This publication represents the opinions and views of the author based on his or her personal experience, knowledge, and research. The information in this book serves as a general guide only. The author and publisher have used their best efforts in preparing this book and disclaim liability rising directly or indirectly from the use and application of this book.

CPSIA Compliance Information: Batch #WW15CSQ

All websites were available and accurate when this book was sent to press.

Library of Congress Cataloging-in-Publication Data

Gullo, Arthur, author.
Volcanoes / Arthur Gullo.
pages cm. — (The power of nature)
Includes bibliographical references and index.
ISBN 978-1-50260-221-3 (hardcover) ISBN 978-1-50260-220-6 (ebook)
1. Volcanoes—Juvenile literature. 2. Volcanologists—Juvenile literature. I. Title.

QE521.3.G85 2015
551.21—dc23

2014019950

Editor: Fletcher Doyle
Copy Editor: Cynthia Roby
Art Director: Jeffrey Talbot
Designer: Joseph Macri
Senior Production Manager: Jennifer Ryder-Talbot
Production Editor: David McNamara
Photo Researcher: J8 Media

Printed in the United States of America

CONTENTS

INTRODUCTION 5

CHAPTER ONE   FORMATION OF A VOLCANO   9

CHAPTER TWO   RANGE OF ERUPTIONS   19

CHAPTER THREE   KEEPING WATCH ON VOLCANOES   29

GLOSSARY   40

FURTHER INFORMATION   43

INDEX   46

Volcanic ash from the eruption of Eyjafjallajökull in 2010 distrupted European air travel for a month.

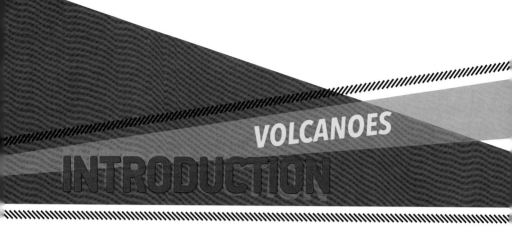

When Iceland's volcano Eyjafjallajökull (pronounced AY-yah-fyat-lay-uh-kuh-tl) erupted in March 2010, it didn't cause much of a reaction on the tiny island. Iceland is home to many **active** volcanoes, and by their standards, the event was relatively small.

The volcano's plume climbed no more than about 7 miles (11.3 kilometers) into the sky, and it released about 9.5 billion cubic feet (270 million cubic meters) of ash over several months. This is less than some **eruptions** can spew out in a day.

The ash cloud, however, traveled great distances and caused airports to shut down all over Europe. Airplanes were not allowed to fly because the fine particles of dust could damage their engines. Millions of passengers were stranded as flights from major cities such as Paris and London were grounded, and no planes were allowed into these important hubs. The loss in airline ticket sales was estimated at $200 million each day. That small volcano caused big problems.

What is a volcano, though?

A volcano is an opening in the Earth's surface. Volcanoes allow hot, liquid rock from inside Earth to escape. Ash, solid rock, and gases may also be released. When this hot matter pours or shoots out of a volcano, it is

Eyjafjallajökull's eruption sent ash into the atmosphere from April 14, 2010 until May 23, 2010.

called an eruption.

Most volcanoes are mountains. These mountains form when hot, liquid rock, called **lava**, cools around the volcano's opening. With each eruption, layers of hardened lava build up. As more eruptions occur over time, a volcano can grow bigger and bigger.

Eyjafjallajökull had not erupted since 1821, but it is part of a chain that is responsible for the existence of the island. It is one of the youngest landmasses on Earth. It was formed because of a large volcanic **hot spot** created by a fissure in the Mid-Atlantic Ridge.

There are 169 active volcanoes in the United States and more than 1,500 worldwide. Most are found on the Ring of Fire around the Pacific Ocean. Some volcanoes remain inactive for centuries, and some erupt nearly every day. In this book, you will explore different kinds of volcanoes, how they form, the deadliest eruptions, and the most active sites.

Plaster casts were made of thirteen victims in the Garden of the Fugitives in Pompeii.

The most famous volcanic eruption took place in an area known today as Italy. Two cities, Pompeii and Herculaneum, lay at the foot of Mount Vesuvius. On August 24, in 79 CE, Mount Vesuvius shot out ash and rock with so much force that it shot 12 miles (19 km) into the sky. When all this ash and rock fell, all of Pompeii was buried beneath it.

Next, Vesuvius spewed a flood of lava upon Herculaneum. People tried running toward the Bay of Naples but were unable to escape this river of fire. More than 20 feet (6 m) of volcanic rock smothered the city.

It was once widely assumed that most of Vesuvius's victims suffocated in volcanic ash and gas. Scientists now believe that unbearable temperatures, more than 300 degrees Celsius (572 degrees Fahrenheit), killed the people of Pompeii instantly. In 1748, hollow impressions of their bodies were found in the hardened volcanic debris, which showed they died while doing ordinary things. Using these impressions, scientists were able to create body casts from plaster.

How Volcanoes Form

Earth is made up of three layers: the **crust**, the **mantle,** and the **core**. The crust is the top layer. It can measure from 4 to 43 miles (6 to 69 km) thick. The crust is broken into large pieces of rock, called **plates**. Plates move very slowly over Earth's middle layer, called the mantle. The mantle makes up nearly 80 percent of Earth's size. It is about 1,800 miles (2,898 km) thick. The mantle surrounds Earth's center, or core.

Core temperatures reach 6,700°F (3,704°C). At such temperatures, rock melts. It turns into **molten**, or liquid-hot rock. This molten rock is called **magma**. The mantle is made up of solid rock, but it has pockets of magma, too. Volcanoes are formed when magma from within Earth's upper mantle works its way to the surface.

Magma rises toward the crust, cools, and sinks back down. This circular movement underneath the plates causes them to move.

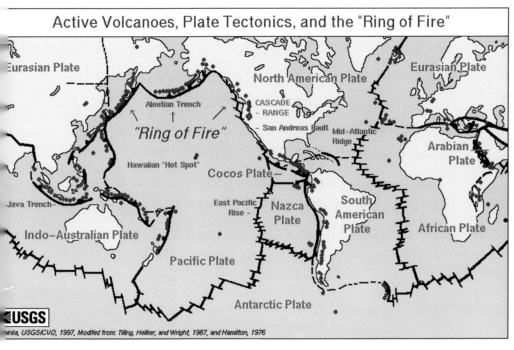

Active Volcanoes, Plate Tectonics, and the "Ring of Fire"

Eurasian Plate

North American Plate

Eurasian Plate

Aleutian Trench

CASCADE - RANGE

"Ring of Fire"

San Andreas Fault

Mid-Atlantic Ridge

Arabian Plate

Hawaiian "Hot Spot"

Cocos Plate

Java Trench

East Pacific Rise

Nazca Plate

South American Plate

African Plate

Indo-Australian Plate

Pacific Plate

Antarctic Plate

USGS

ninka, USGS/CVO, 1997, Modified from: Tilling, Heliker, and Wright, 1987, and Hamilton, 1976

Red spots on the map above mark the locations of active volcanoes. They are found where two tectonic plates meet, mostly around the Pacific Plate.

The movement is slow and takes place over millions of years.

As the plates move, they rub against each other. Magma pushes up through spaces in the crust where plates meet. This is where many volcanoes form. Magma can also melt through the middle of a plate. This kind of volcano is called a hot spot.

As rock turns into magma, it gives off hot gas. The most common volcanic gases are carbon dioxide, water vapor, sulfur dioxide,

11

and hydrogen sulfide. Gases rise when they become hot. The underground gas pushes its way out of the mantle through underground passages that lead up to Earth's crust. The hot gas pushes magma up with it, too. Once in the crust, the gas and magma collect in pockets called **magma chambers**. Sometimes the pressure in these chambers can become too great. Then it forces the magma and gas out

DID YOU KNOW?

Mount Everest is the world's tallest mountain when measured from sea level. However, Mauna Loa, a volcano in Hawai'i, is actually much taller than Mount Everest. Much of its height is underwater, however. From its base to its peak it stands at about 56,000 feet (17,000 m). This is more than 27,000 feet (8,230 m) taller than Mount Everest. However, since only about 13,680 feet (4,170 m) of its height is above sea level, Mount Everest is considered taller.

Earth's layers are its inner core, outer core, lower mantle, upper mantle, and crust.

through **fissures**, or cracks in Earth's surface. These openings are called **vents**.

Magma that escapes onto the Earth's surface is called lava. Sometimes lava is thin and runny. Other times it is thick and gooey. **Lava flows** have been known to travel at speeds of more than 80 miles per hour (129 kilometers per hour). Some lava flows cover more than 100 square miles (259 sq. km) of land.

Volcanic eruptions often send many tiny pieces of dust and ash into the air. Volcanic dust particles measure less than 0.01 inch (0.25 millimeters) in diameter. These particles are so fine that they remain in the air for a long time. The ash from eruptions are burnt splinters that measure less than 0.2 inches (5 mm) in diameter. Ash is heavier than dust, and so it falls to the ground. Then it mixes with lava and mud.

Volcano Types

There are two types of volcanoes: **fissure volcanoes** and central volcanoes. The shape of a volcano and the way it erupts determine its type.

Fissure volcanoes form when lava comes out of long fissures in the crust. These fissures can be many miles long, so lava spreads over a large area. When the lava cools, it forms a plain of volcanic rock.

Central volcanoes form when lava comes out of one large, central vent. There are many different types of central volcanoes, including cinder cones, composites, domes, and shields.

Cinder cones resemble low, wide mountains with their tops sliced off. They form when ash and cinders escape the vent.

Composite volcanoes rise as high as 8,000 feet (2,438 m) from a wide base to a small,

Lava flows from the vents in Mount Etna on December 16, 2013.

round vent that has even smaller openings around it. Some examples of composite volcanoes are Mount Fuji in Japan, Mount Etna in Italy, and Mount St. Helens in the United States. Dome volcanoes are steep and rounded. They form when thick lava pours out of the vent and cools quickly.

Shield volcanoes are low and dome-shaped, but differ from dome volcanoes because they are spread over a large area. All of these volcanoes are capable of causing a lot of damage.

GLOBAL COOLING

Mary Shelley created the creature Frankenstein while stranded in this home on Lake Geneva in Switzerland.

Volcanic eruptions can affect people very far away from the place where the eruptions happen. The year 1816 was called "The Year Without Summer" due to freezing temperatures in some parts of the world during the late spring and summer. Scientists now believe the cause was the eruption of Mount Tambora on Sumbawa Island (now a part of Indonesia), which took place on April 15, 1815. The weeklong eruption spewed an estimated 1.7 million tons (1.54 million metric tons) of ash.

In Indonesia, seventy thousand to ninety thousand people died from the effects of the volcano. Many died from famine when the ash poisoned their crops.

When that airborne ash reached the Northern Hemisphere, it blocked the sun, causing temperatures to drop. The temperature loss was 3° to 6°F (1.7° to 3.4°C), but there was frost every month during the growing season, which caused crops to wither. Hardest hit were New England, the Atlantic provinces of Canada, and parts of Western Europe, which suffered its last general famine. It rained 130 of 152 days in Switzerland. Lord Byron, Mary Shelley, and others were stranded in their villa near Lake Geneva. They passed the time by seeing who could write the best ghost story. It was then that Shelley produced the classic *Frankenstein*.

Harvests were reduced in the United States, and the prices on some goods tripled. Farmers sold their livestock because they couldn't feed them. The weather conditions were also blamed for a worldwide cholera epidemic in 1817.

The eruption of Martinique's Mount Pelée in 1902 completely destroyed the city of St. Pierre.

When Mount Pelée, located on the Caribbean island of Martinique, erupted in 1902, it killed more people than any volcano in the twentieth century. Although **dormant** for hundreds of years, it had given many warnings that it was about to erupt.

For more than a week in April that year, Mount Pelée sent ash into the air. The sky above the island turned dark during the daytime. The streets of the nearby city of St. Pierre were being covered with ash. Minor earthquakes shook the island.

Some people began to flee, boarding boats to get off the island. Yet many St. Pierre residents felt there was nothing to worry about. These events happened before and the volcano had not erupted. This time, however, it did.

On the morning of May 8, 1902, Mount Pelée exploded with full force, sending a huge cloud of volcanic material rocketing into the air. A second burst quickly followed. Lava flowed down the sides of the mountain toward St. Pierre at a speed of 100 miles per hour (161 kilometers per hour). In just minutes, thirty thousand people were buried underneath burning rock and ash.

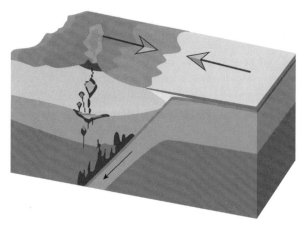

In a subduction zone, one tectonic plate dives beneath another and, at a certain depth, forms the magma that builds volcanoes.

Mount Pelée is located in a subduction zone. In a subduction zone, one of the Earth's plates moves under another, curving down into the mantle. The mantle is the hotter layer. In this kind of zone, gases can escape. The gases partly melt the crust to form magma, which then creates volcanoes. Mount Pelée has erupted more than thirty times in the last five thousand years.

The world's largest volcano was discovered in 2013. Tamu Massif, believed to be about 145 million years old, lies underwater one thousand miles east of Japan. It covers 120,000 square miles (311,000 sq. km), which is the size of New Mexico. The largest active volcano, Mauna Loa in Hawai'i, covers 2,000 square miles (5,200 sq. km).

Types of Eruptions

There are six different types of volcanic eruptions. Each is based on the strength of the eruption. From weakest to strongest, these are: Icelandic, Hawai'ian, Strombolian, Vulcanian, Peléan, and Plinian.

Icelandic and Hawai'ian

When eruptions happen in Iceland or Hawai'i, they are generally considered minor eruptions. In both places, lava oozes slowly from fissures.

Icelandic eruptions happen in fissure volcanoes. Hawai'ian eruptions happen in central volcanoes. Lava from Hawai'ian eruptions flows down mountainsides as hot fudge does over ice cream. Both types are named after places where they are common, although Icelandic and Hawai'ian eruptions can happen throughout the world.

Lava at Hawai'i Volcanoes National Park flows in the ocean.

Strombolian and Vulcanian

Many eruptions happen through a vent, or an opening in Earth's crust. During Strombolian and Vulcanian eruptions, thick lava blocks the vent and prevents hot gases from escaping. Pressure builds up until gas, lava, and solid rock shoot out of the vent.

Vulcanian eruptions are stronger than are Strombolians, and often produce dark clouds of ash and rock. These two types of eruptions are named after Stromboli and Vulcano, two volcanic islands in Italy.

Peléan and Plinian

Peléan eruptions spew thick mixtures of lava, rock, and gas into the air. Peléans are so strong that they often force part of the mountain to explode.

Plinian eruptions are the strongest type of eruptions. During a Plinian eruption, the center of the volcano explodes. A mushroom-shaped cloud rises from the volcano. This cloud can hang over an area for several hours. The eruption of Vesuvius in 79 CE was a Plinian blast.

Mount Tambora now rests peacefully on Sumbawa Island.

It is impossible to determine the biggest eruptions in history. These volcanoes are ranked by estimates of the number of people who died.

1. **Mount Tambora, Indonesia, 1815; Death Toll: 92,000** Ten times greater than Krakatoa's eruption.

2. **Krakatoa, Indonesia, 1883; Death Toll: 36,000** Equaled thirteen thousand atomic bombs.

3. **Mount Pelée, Martinique, 1902; Death Toll: 29,000** St. Pierre was destroyed.

4. **Nevado del Ruiz, Colombia, 1985; Death Toll: 23,000** The second-deadliest eruption of the twentieth century.

5. **Mount Unzen, Japan, 1792; Death Toll: 14,300** The eruption set off a deadly tsunami.

6. **Laki, Iceland, 1783; Death Toll: 9,350** Most starved to death as agriculture failed.

7. **Kilat, Indonesia, 1919; Death Toll: 5,100** Eruption in 1586 killed more than ten thousand.

8. **Mount Galunggung, Indonesia, 1882, Death Toll: 4,011** In its largest eruption, 114 villages were destroyed.

9. **Mount Vesuvius, Italy, 1631; Death Toll: 3,500** Eruption in 79 CE killed 3,360.

10. **Papandayan, Indonesia, 1772; Death Toll: 2957** Forty villages were wiped out.

Source: Volcano World

A pyroclastic flow in 2009 shows Krakatoa is still alive 150 years after its massive eruption.

Rivers of Fire

Explosive eruptions, especially Vulcanian and Peléan blasts, spew chunks of earth into the sky. Large eruptions produce rivers of fiery rock. These volcanic floods are called **pyroclastic flows**. Pyroclastic flows as hot as 1,470°F (799°C) can pour downhill at speeds of 200 miles per hour (322 kmh). Unlucky victims are likely to be burned or even crushed by pyroclastic flows.

Pyroclastic flows are made up of heavy rock. They can only flow downhill from the volcano.

Sometimes, however, pyroclastic material mixes with a lot of hot gas. If enough gas mixes with the pyroclastic rock, the gas-rock mixture can travel uphill. This combination of rock and gas is called a **pyroclastic surge**.

Calderas

The biggest eruptions are so huge they can spew out hundreds of cubic miles of lava. Such a giant eruption leaves an empty pocket underneath the volcano. After the eruption, the volcano collapses into the empty space beneath it. This creates a huge depression in the land, called a **caldera**. Some calderas can be 15 miles (24 km) wide and several miles deep. Often, rainwater can collect in a caldera and form a lake. Crater Lake (above) in southwestern Oregon is a famous example of a caldera lake.

Volcanologist David Johnston descends into the Mount St. Helens crater lake to collect samples on April 30, 1980. He died that day while manning an observation post during the volcano's eruption.

Most eruptions cannot be predicted, but volcanoes may give warning signs before they erupt. Sometimes a volcano will grow slightly larger before it erupts. This growth is caused by the magma that collects underneath it. The temperature around the volcano may increase and steam may pour from its vent.

Scientists called volcanologists use different tools to predict eruptions. They use a **tiltmeter** to measure the size of a volcano, a thermometer to check for increases in temperature, and gas detectors to detect volcanic gas. A **seismograph** is used to measure vibrations underneath volcano areas. Earthquakes often happen along with eruptions. If a seismograph picks up movement of the earth, it may be a sign the volcano above will erupt soon.

In the late 1970s, two scientists studied volcanic rock around Mount St. Helens in

David Johnston uses a spectrometer to measure the content of gases coming out of Mount St. Helens six weeks before the eruption.

Washington state, a volcano that had last erupted in 1857. In 1978, the scientists released a report that said the volcano could erupt before the end of the century. Officials warned residents to leave the area, and Mount St. Helens was closed to the public.

Scientists continued to study the volcano. On the morning of May 18, 1980, Dr. David Johnston was collecting data on Mount St. Helens from an observation post 6 miles (9.7 km) away. Just after 8:30 a.m., the volcano exploded in a huge Plinian eruption.

Volcanic matter shot 15 miles (24 km) into the sky in less than thirty minutes. The explosion spewed out 20-foot (6-m) boulders. Rivers of mud and volcanic rock 50 feet (15 m) deep poured down the mountain at speeds of 90 miles per hour (145 kmh). This made the mountain 1,314 feet (400.5 m) shorter. The mountain caved in, forming a crater 2,084 feet (635.2 m) deep, 1.8 miles (2.9 km) long, and 1.3 miles (2.1 km) wide. Air that was heated to 660°F (348.9°C) blasted north, carrying rocks and debris at 650 miles per hour (1,046 kmh). The blast ripped out trees by their roots, devastating 150,000 acres (60,703 hectares)

Lassen Peak is a sleeping volcano.

of forest. Dr. Johnston was one of fifty-seven people who died in the eruption.

Active Volcanoes

Scientists have four different categories in which to classify volcanic activity. They classify volcanoes as active, **intermittent**, dormant, and **extinct**.

A volcano that erupts often over long periods of time is called an active volcano. Stromboli is a volcanic island near Italy that has been erupting on a regular basis for several years. This volcano is known as "the lighthouse of the Mediterranean Sea" because it is always glowing. Stromboli erupts nearly every twenty minutes.

Intermittent Volcanoes

An intermittent volcano erupts much less often than one that is active. Each eruption is followed by a "down time" in which the volcano is not erupting. A down time may last anywhere from a few months to one hundred years.

Dormant Volcanoes

A dormant volcano is a volcano that is not active but has the possibility to become active again. Dormant volcanoes also are called sleeping volcanoes. Lassen Peak in California, and Mount Rainier in Washington are dormant volcanoes.

Extinct Volcanoes

An extinct volcano is one that has not been active for thousands of years. There are hundreds of extinct volcanoes all over the world. Scientists are confident that these volcanoes will never erupt again.

Mount Rainier looms above Seattle.

There are only six hundred active volcanoes on Earth. As many as sixty-eight are in the United States. Around fourty-eight of these are found in Alaska and Hawai'i, and twenty are located within the contiguous United States. Only Japan and Indonesia have more active volcanoes than the United States. Here are some of America's most dangerous volcanoes:

Mount Rainier, Washington
Mount Rainier is a 14,411-foot (4,392-m) active volcano that looms above Seattle, Washington.

It is one of several volcanoes in the Cascade mountain range. Seven volcanoes have erupted in the Cascades in the past two hundred years. Mount Rainier last erupted in 1882. Its next eruption could threaten Seattle.

Kilauea and Mauna Loa, Hawai'i

The Hawai'i Volcanoes National Park boasts some of the world's most frightening volcanoes. Kilauea is 50 miles (80 km) long and 14 miles (23 km) wide. It has experienced a series of small eruptions since 1983. Kilauea lies to the southeast of a bigger volcano, Mauna Loa. Mauna Loa is 70 miles (113 km) long and 30,000 feet (9144 m) high, making it the largest active volcano on the planet. In 1984, its lava flow reached to within 4 miles (6.4 km) of the city of Hilo.

Mount Hood, Oregon

Standing at 11,237 feet (3,425 m), Mount Hood is the tallest mountain in Oregon. It is also a volcano. Mount Hood is popular with skiers, hikers, and rock climbers. Its last series of eruptions occurred 180 to 250 years ago.

The **Volcanic Explosivity Index (VEI)** measures eruptions on a scale of 0 to 8 based on different factors. The 1815 eruption in Tambora, Indonesia, is estimated not only to have rated 7 on the index, but also to have ejected as much as eighty times more ash than did the Mount St. Helens eruption, which had a rating of 5.

Dangers

Lava, flying rock, and deadly temperatures are not the only dangers associated with volcanic eruptions. Volcanic ash can travel for hundreds or even thousands of miles from the eruption site. As it spreads through the atmosphere, this ash makes it difficult, or sometimes impossible, to see or breathe. It pollutes drinking water and kills plants. If the ash is thick and heavy enough, it can cause the roofs of structures to collapse. Clouds of ash can clog jet and car engines, making it difficult for officials to search an area for survivors.

Eruptions release huge clouds of gas that can sometimes cause people to **suffocate**. These gas clouds can even be poisonous, made up of deadly gases such as hydrogen sulfide, carbon monoxide, carbon dioxide, and sulfur dioxide. In August 1986, a caldera in Cameroon, West Africa, released a cloud of carbon dioxide that killed 1,700 people.

Staying Safe

Millions of Americans live in areas that could be affected by eruptions. If you are one of these people, you should remember these safety tips:

- Do not hike on or go near an active volcano, even if it's not erupting.

- Put together an emergency kit that includes goggles, a mask, a flashlight, and a working radio with batteries.

- Keep gas in your car and know your evacuation route. Avoid rivers and other low-lying areas, and take only those routes recommended by authorities.

- Take volcano warnings seriously. Close all windows and vents in your home and change into long-sleeved clothing. Don't wear contact lenses.

There is not much you can do if a volcano erupts without warning. However, if you follow these tips, you will give yourself a chance to stay safe as you respect the awesome power of volcanoes.

Lava lakes inside the Ambrym volcano in the
Republic of Vanuatu attract both adventurers
and researchers.

active A volcano that erupts continuously over long periods of time.

caldera A huge depression at the top of a collapsed volcano, sometimes confused with volcanic craters.

core The center of Earth.

crust The top layer of Earth.

dormant When a volcano has not erupted for a long time, it is said to be dormant.

eruption When lava, rocks, and ash pour out of a volcano.

extinct When a volcano will never again erupt.

fissures The cracks in the Earth's surface.

fissure volcano A volcano in which lava oozes from a long fissure.

hot spot An area where magma seeps through the crust and volcanoes are formed.

intermittent When a volcano erupts off and on.

lava Melted rock after it flows or shoots out of a volcano; aboveground magma.

lava flow The movement of hot lava over Earth's surface.

magma Melted rock below Earth's surface; it turns into lava when it moves above ground.

magma chamber A large section beneath the crust where magma collects.

mantle The middle layer of Earth.

molten Rock that is melted, or liquid-hot.

plates Huge sections of rock that make up Earth's crust.

pyroclastic flow A flood of volcanic rock.

pyroclastic surge A rising mixture of volcanic rock and gas.

seismograph A tool that records earthquake waves.

suffocate The inability to breathe caused by a lack of oxygen.

tiltmeter A tool that measures the size of a volcano.

vent An opening in a volcano through which magma escapes.

Volcanic Explosivity Index (VEI) A scale used to grade volcanic eruptions.

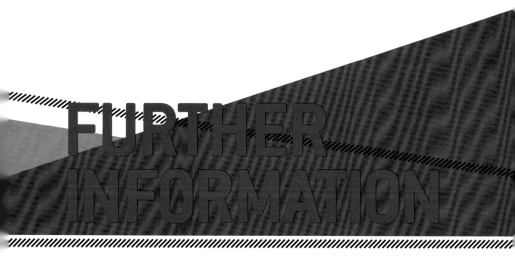

Books

Griffey, Harriet. *Eyewitness Readers: Volcanoes and Other Natural Disasters.* New York, NY: DK Publishing, 1998.

Heiken, Grant. *Dangerous Neighbors: Volcanoes and Cities.* Cambridge, UK: Cambridge University Press, 2013.

Klingamen, William K., and Nicholas P. Klingaman. *The Year Without Summer: 1816 and the Volcano That Darkened the World and Changed History.* New York, NY: St. Martin's Press, 2013.

van Rose, Susanna. *Volcanoes and Earthquakes.* New York, NY: DK Children, 2014.

Wood, Gillen D'Arcy. *Tambora: The Eruption That Changed the World.* Princeton, NJ: Princeton University Press, 2014.

Websites

Global Vulcanism Report
volcano.si.edu/reports_weekly.cfm
Updated every Wednesday, this site documents, updates, and disseminates information about global volcanic activity. Students can access educational information on eruptions including blogs and videos.

Hawai'i Volcanoes National Park
nps.gov/havo/index.htm
Take a look at the park's archives and view extensive documentaries that explore volcanic eruptions. Plan a trip to the park or take a virtual hike through many of its trails.

Hawai'i National Geographic Fun Science, Volcanoes 101

video.nationalgeographic.com/video/101-videos/volcanoes-101

Search the chronicles and explore a number of educational videos and spectacular images of volcanoes worldwide.

Volcano World

volcano.oregonstate.edu

Learn what it's like to work on an active volcano. Explore science lessons and learn more about prehistoric Earth, and read interviews with volcanologists from many countries.

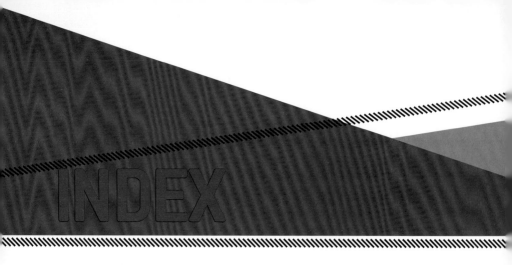

INDEX

Page numbers
in **boldface** are
illustrations.

active volcano, 5, 7,
 11, 21, 32, 34–35,
 37, 45

caldera(s), 27, 37
Cascade mountain
 range, 35
central volcano(es),
 14, 22
cinder cone(s), 14
composite(s), 14
core, 10, **13**
crust, 10–14, 20, 23

deadly gas clouds, 37
dome(s), 14–15
dormant, 19, 32, 33

extinct, 32, 33

fissure(s), 7, 12, 14,
 21–22
fissure volcano(es),
 14, 22

Hawai´i Volcanoes
 National Park,
 22, 35
Hawaiian eruptions,
 21–22, 35
Herculaneum, 9
hot spot, 7, 11

Icelandic eruptions,
   21–22
intermittent, 32

Kilauea, 35
Krakatoa, Indonesia,
   24, **26**

lava, 7, 9, 13–15,
   20–23, 27, 36
lava flows, 13, **15**,
   35, **39**

magma, 10–13, 20,
   29
magma chambers, 12
mantle, 10, 12, **13**,
   20

Mauna Loa, 12, 21,
   35
molten, 10
Mount Etna, **15**
Mount Fuji, 15
Mount Hood, 35
Mount Pelée,
   18, 19–20, 24
Mount Rainier,
   33, 34–35
Mount St. Helens,
   15, **28**, **30**,
   31–32, 36
Mount Vesuvius,
   9, 25

Peléan eruption(s), 23

plates, 10–11, 20

plinian eruption(s), 23, 31

Pompeii, **8**, 9–10

pyroclastic flows, 26

pyroclastic surge, 27

seismograph(s), 29, 31

shield(s), 14, 15

Strombolian eruption(s), 21, 23, 32

tiltmeter, 29

vent, 12, 14, **15**, 23, 29, 38

Volcanic Explosivity Index (VEI), 36

volcanologists, **28**, 29

Vulcanian eruption(s), 23